SCHOOLS

By Joanna Brundle

KidHaven
PUBLISHING

A Look at Life
Around the World

Published in 2019 by
KidHaven Publishing, an Imprint of Greenhaven Publishing, LLC
353 3rd Avenue
Suite 255
New York, NY 10010

Designer: Jasmine Pointer
Editor: Kirsty Holmes

Photocredits: Abbreviations: l-left, r-right, b-bottom, t-top, c-center, m-middle. All images are courtesy of Shutterstock.com. With thanks to Getty Images, Thinkstock Photo and iStockphoto. Front cover - CRS PHOTO, Monkey Business Images, jianbing Lee. 2 - CRS PHOTO. 4t - Andrei Kholmov. 4b - Dennis Wegewijs. 5 - Grigvovan. 6 - Mr.Note19. 7t - Vladimir Zhoga. 7b - Georgy Golovin. 8l - CRS PHOTO. 8r - A_Lesik. 9l - CECIL BO DZWOWA. 9r - CRS PHOTO. 10t - humphery. 10b - Elena Nasledova. 11t - David Jallaud. 11b - Dewi Putra. 12 - jianbing Lee. 13 - lazyllama. 14 - Somchai Sanvongchaiya. 15t - Nach-Noth. 15b - Click Images. 16 - Photographee.eu. 17t - Tupungato. 17b - Ruslan Harutyunov. 18t - juri um. 18b - Tropical studio. 19 - Svet_Feo. 20 - XiXinXing. 21 - espies. 21b - iceink. 22t - Adwo. 22b - alionabirukova.

Cataloging-in-Publication Data

Names: Brundle, Joanna.
Title: Schools / Joanna Brundle.
Description: New York : KidHaven Publishing, 2019. | Series: A look at life around the world | Includes glossary and index.
Identifiers: ISBN 9781534528352 (pbk.) | ISBN 9781534528376 (library bound) | ISBN 9781534528369 (6 pack) | ISBN 9781534528383 (ebook)
Subjects: LCSH: Schools--Juvenile literature.
Classification: LCC LB1556.B78 2019 | DDC 371--dc23

Printed in the United States of America

CPSIA compliance information: Batch #BW19KL: For further information contact Greenhaven Publishing LLC, New York, New York at 1-844-317-7404.

Please visit our website, www.greenhavenpublishing.com. For a free color catalog of all our high-quality books, call toll free 1-844-317-7404 or fax 1-844-317-7405.

CONTENTS

Words that look like this can be found in the glossary on page 23.

ALL KINDS OF SCHOOLS

Have you ever wondered what it might be like to go to school in another country? In this book, we will be traveling around the world, finding out. As you read, think about how the schools we visit are similar to your school and how they are different.

This brightly colored school is in Russia.

There are 120 pupils in each class at this school in Uganda.

There are very few children in this Russian classroom.

Some schools are huge with thousands of pupils. Others are very small. Some have <u>resources</u> like laptops, while others have no electricity or books. Around the world, there are schools in unusual places – in caves, on boats, and in old castles and churches. Whatever and wherever they are, all schools help children like you to learn new skills.

GETTING TO SCHOOL

Most children in India walk to school or ride the bus. However, some children ride a three-wheel bicycle taxi called a rickshaw.

Some children have to walk long distances to get to school. Some, like these little boys in Nepal, walk on their own. Sometimes, older children look after the younger ones.

Nenets are people from the freezing north of Russia. They herd reindeer. When winter comes, Nenets children travel by helicopter to a <u>boarding school</u>. They stay at the boarding school for up to nine months.

How do you get to school? How long does your journey take?

SCHOOL BUILDINGS AND EQUIPMENT

This school in India has a computer room.

This school in Ukraine has a theater where the children can perform plays and music.

Some schools have clean, modern classrooms with plenty of space. They may have a <u>gymnasium</u>, music rooms, art studios, and playing fields. Many have computer rooms and a cafeteria. They have heating for the winter and air conditioning for the summer.

Some schools have only basic classrooms with no computers or writing equipment. Some students have their lessons outside. If there are no desks, students sit on the floor for lessons. Some children are <u>refugees</u>. They live in refugee camps, where basic schools are set up in tents.

The children in this school in Zimbabwe share a computer.

Lessons at this school in India take place outdoors.

UNIFORMS

The children wear a red scarf to represent the Chinese flag.

Children in Australia wear hats as part of their uniform, to protect them from the hot sun.

In China, children have formal uniforms for special occasions, but their everyday uniform looks like a tracksuit. In Japan, children wear white slippers called uwabaki in school to keep their classrooms clean. In Sri Lanka, girls wear a white dress with a tie. It must be hard to keep clean!

In Bhutan, the school uniform for girls and boys is a long robe called a gho. Girls also wear a rectangular piece of cloth called a kira over the top.

The gho is tied at the waist with a belt and looks a bit like a bathrobe.

White Headscarf

Some school uniforms reflect religious beliefs.

THE SCHOOL DAY

Chinese schools have a ceremony each day in which the national flag is raised and the <u>national anthem</u> is played.

Children in China have one of the longest school days, starting at 7:15 a.m. and finishing at 4:15 p.m. Before classes, they perform eye exercises to music to protect their eyesight. They also do daily physical exercises – loudspeakers give out instructions.

BREAK TIME

At break time, children rush to eat and play. In Egypt, school stops for a midmorning breakfast of pita bread and beans. Soccer is a popular playground game everywhere, especially in Brazil. In India, children play rumaal chor or hanky thief, taking the piece of cloth in turns to chase the thief.

In hot countries like Spain, children have a three-hour break called a siesta, returning to school from 3 to 5 p.m.

In some countries, children work during the day, earning money to help their families. This stops some children from going to school at all, but some manage to attend school in the evenings.

This little girl works on a tobacco farm.

In South Korea, children who have been at school all day return in the evening to do even more schoolwork.

HOME TIME

In Japan, children clean their classrooms every day before they go home. They sweep the floor, tidy up, and clean the toilets. Japanese schools teach children that it is important to work together and take care of your things.

Schools in many places offer after-school clubs. Activities include sports, dance, chess, and crafts.

Do you go to any after-school clubs? Do you have a favorite one?

This little boy in Russia is learning to play ice hockey.

LESSONS

All over the world, children learn math, reading and writing, and science. Many learn a foreign language, too. Children who have <u>emigrated</u> from another country have special lessons to help them learn the language of their new country. In Bashkiria, schoolchildren learn beekeeping and many schools have their own hives.

These students in the United States are learning Spanish.

soleado

Parcialmente nublado

nublado

la lluvia

la nieve

aguanieve

El tornado

In Japan, children have classes in which they learn how to be good people and <u>respect</u> others. They also have lessons to teach them how to enjoy the beauty of nature.

Traditional dancing is an important lesson in schools in Armenia. Armenian people are very proud of their traditional dances and costumes.

Music is taught in many schools. Children learn to sing traditional songs and play instruments. In Korea, children are taught to play a traditional drum called a janggu.

In Australia and Hawaii, children are lucky enough to have lessons at the beach! The <u>curriculum</u> in these places includes surfing.

Some children have a special <u>talent</u> and go to a school that helps them to develop their talent. At a ballet school, children have ordinary lessons but also spend several hours each day in dance classes. Some go on to become professional dancers.

These young dancers go to a ballet school in Russia.

FOOD AT SCHOOL

These children in China are having a noodle stir-fry for lunch.

Some schools have a cafeteria serving hot lunches. In Uganda, matoke is a popular lunch dish. It is a savory banana that is cooked and mashed with tomato sauce. In Japan, many children eat a packed lunch from a bento box. Parents may make faces and patterns with the food inside.

In India, Malaysia, Thailand, and Singapore, children take a packed lunch to school in a tiffin box. These boxes are made up of metal pans that stack together. The largest pan at the bottom contains rice. Other layers contain lentils, spicy meat, and a flat bread called a chapati.

The metal clasps at the side hold all the layers together.

Tiffin boxes come in lots of different shapes and colors.

UNUSUAL SCHOOLS

River Plate Stadium

The River Plate Stadium in Buenos Aires, Argentina, is home to the national soccer team. It also has a school for 2,000 children.

Zhongdong is a village inside the Zhong caves in China. The school is thought to be the only cave school in the world.

Chong Khneas is a floating village on Lake Tonle Sap in Cambodia. The village includes floating homes, shops, and schools.

GLOSSARY

boarding school   a school where pupils eat and sleep, only returning home for the holidays

curriculum   a list of subjects that pupils must study in a particular place

emigrated   left a country to live in a different country

gymnasium   a room or building for indoor sports and exercise

national anthem   a song played or sung at important events to show love for a country

refugees   people who have been forced to leave their homes to escape danger

resources   things that are of use or value

respect   consider the feelings, values, wishes, and rights of other people

talent   a natural ability to do well in a particular activity

INDEX